MAUD ALCORN

Black Girl Flesh

A collection of Poems, Quotes, and Micro-Essays

First published by Malaysia Alcorn 2020

Copyright © 2020 by Maud Alcorn

All rights reserved. No part of this publication may be reproduced, stored or transmitted in any form or by any means, electronic, mechanical, photocopying, recording, scanning, or otherwise without written permission from the publisher. It is illegal to copy this book, post it to a website, or distribute it by any other means without permission.

Maud Alcorn has no responsibility for the persistence or accuracy of URLs for external or third-party Internet Websites referred to in this publication and does not guarantee that any content on such Websites is, or will remain, accurate or appropriate.

First edition

ISBN: 978-1-7351160-0-6

This book was professionally typeset on Reedsy. Find out more at reedsy.com

To every body that holds this book,
I pray it holds you back.
With big love,
& big gratitude.
- Maud

Contents

Preface   v
Note From the Author   vii
blak gərl fleSH   viii

I   Flesh

The Courage to Stand Up Straight	3
Confetti	5
Living in the Belly of a Beast	6
Backstroke	8
C/eserean	9
Quarter Breath	12
Miss. Luis Land	13
On a Sunday, or Monday	15
Can't Ring Me Up	16
It's In You	17
Textured Skin	18
A Bag Full of Bricks	20

II   Blood

Stone Fruit	25
Abyss	27
Luther Let Me Sang	28
Fairy Tales for Black Girls	30
Amerikkkan Pie	31
The Collective	33
I Really Am Just Human	34
Cycles of The Moon	35
My Own Wonderland	36
Cast a Spell When I Want To	38
Gore, Wetness, & Weeping	39
With My Own Permission	41

III   Body

The Audacity of This...	45
Frame Me Free	47
Homebound	48
The Good Steward	51
Swallow Whole	52
Infinite Me	53
Veins Be a Wiretap	54
Watch Me Riot	56
My Body Bag	57
#FreeMyWords	59
Dancing With Two Fat Feet	60
Mental Gymnastics	62

IV Heart

Love, of Course	67
Shrunken	70
Music Holds Memories	71
& Again	73
House of Worship	74
Sweet, Sweet Love	76
Out of My Element	77
It Is My Pleasure	78
Diving In It	79
Rejoice	80
My Own Magic	81
When Flowers Die	83

V Spirit

Last Respects	87
Lay a Rose	88
A Couple Bodies	89
Lost Connection	90
I Could've Been Ugly	91
10 Toes Down	94
[Redacted] Black Woman	95
Sacrifice	96
Joyful, Joyful	97
Gut Full of Happiness	98
The Void of Loss	99
Hair Heavy	101

VI   The End

A Completed Cycle   105
Give Thanks   106
About the Author   107

Preface

Before I was strong or resilient. Before I knew endurance. Before I was told I was magical, all I had was this body. These bones that keep me standing. This blood that blesses me by running through my veins every day. This spirit that sifts through so much pain just for sliver of joy. This flesh. I was just human. Just woman. Just simply existing. I am praised for being the former, but the latter is somehow lost. Does it hurt the conscience less to hunt down mythical beings, than to see the suffering of the living? Does ones fortified bones make the attempt to break them less evil? Those who will never know this body in consented intimacy, will also never know the difference.

Black Girl Flesh is my own reminder that I am soft. Tender. Tangible. Real. & most of all, human.

A reminder that I exist outside of lustful and exploitative eyes. That when I produce nothing, am nowhere, and drained beyond function, I still am. My existence is my only constant, and pushing it to its limits, or letting it be enough, makes it not feel as heavy as it could. I've had to be my own silver lining. My own breath of fresh air. On some days, I've had to find the why and the why not, and make broken pieces into a life that felt whole.

It all sounds so beautiful, doesn't it? It reads like a poem from a woman who rose from the ashes like a Phoenix. But this is more so the story of the bird who was set aflame, and only got left with 3rd-degree burns. Who had to pick away the burnt skin, and love on the smooth patches where flesh used to be like it still was. Although I can tell the story beautifully, never doubt where it comes from. There is pain here, but I've endured enough pain for this lifetime and the next, so I chose to write about the after.

The after, where the pain is now just a gentle reminder. A gateway. A way out. It grew legs and took off running, and didn't stop until it found turned over land to plant its self in. To grow in. To finally rest and know it would be able to bloom. My pain is now a rose bush. Every spring like clockwork, new blooms in hues of pink and red pop up all over it, and the growing pains become worth it.

I'm one of the lucky ones. My wounds stayed dressed long enough to heal, and when the pain creeped into my mind, those around me made sure to soothe the fire. There were many times I attempted to disown my power, and they read back to me who I was. Malaysia 'Maud' Alcorn. A Black woman so deeply invested in her own healing so others know that it is possible. A Black woman who found her own smile and helps bring one out of others. A Black woman who told the world her body is enough, and if they choose for it not to be, it still is.

This is a collection of poems, quotes, and micro-essays from the life of a Black woman. From her flesh, her blood, her body, her heart, & her spirit. Know that. Cherish that. Honor it by opening yourself up to all of it, in all the ways it will hit you. Yes, there is still magic here, but know that there is also so much more. I pray it finds you well.

Note From the Author

Black Girl Flesh is divided into sections and chapters, but each piece stands alone, and it can be read in any order. Feel free to read it as is, but I urge you to look at the list of pieces, take a deep breath, and read which ever one speaks to you first. I am a strong believer that books, essays, and quotes seek me when I need them. Your spirit will not lie to you. Whichever piece calls out to you, has a message for you. Don't be afraid to receive it.

blak gərl fleSH

/fleSH/
   The skin or surface of the human body with reference to its color, appearance, or sensual properties.
   /fleSH/
   The soft substance consisting of muscle and fat that is found between the skin and bones of an animal or human.
   /fleSH/
   The human body and its physical needs and desires, especially as contrasted with the mind or the soul.
   /fleSH/
   The flesh of an animal, regarded as food.

/blak gərl fleSH/
   Disregarded garbage, to be burned, buried, or never seen again.
   /blak gərl fleSH/
   Hot commodity, only when detached from its original form and worn as costume.
   /blak gərl fleSH/
   The first state of the Black woman before tropes become a noose around her neck.
   /blak gərl fleSH/
   You tell yourself that we are not, to ease your own conscience, but here we are, still.

I

Flesh

The Courage to Stand Up Straight

I got ten toes to stand on.
   A pair of lungs that breathe when they can,
   and two hands that like to hold on too long.
   I got a set of eyes that barely work,
   lips that hold on to each other tightly,
   and a heart that tries to see whatever they can't.
   Got a chest triple-stacked up,
   hips heavily endowed,
   and a tongue so blessed it swims in holy water,
   so every word I speak is anointed.

I got burn marks,
   cut marks,
   and acne marks,
   name a mark and I got it.
   & those are just the ones you see on my skin.
   I wear them all like badges of honor.
   I keep them on display,
   because to hide them,
   would be to hide myself,
   and that I can not do anymore.

BLACK GIRL FLESH

I got patience.
   With myself and those who see light in me.
   With my body that's just learning about stillness,
   and forgiveness,
   & all about love without conditions.
   I have none for anyone telling me to wait for my moment,
   like this ain't my moment,
   like I ain't earn it.
   My time slot on this earth was bought and paid for,
   many moons before my flesh came into play.

I got it all.
   A story worth telling.
   Memories that stretch my mind to hold them.
   I could be a sob story.
   Damn it I am a sob story,
   just one that don't cry for nothing less than joy.
   I don't clap for nothing that turns me into fractions,
   or divides my body into loved and unloved parts.
   Now, I am whole,
   or nothing.
   It is all of me,
   or nothing,
   and never doubt my ability to be alone.

Confetti

"Your mere existence is cause for celebration. You should throw confetti when you walk."

Living in the Belly of a Beast

I don't know where I come from.
    I imagine my birth being like the second big bang,
    and I am the proof that it happened.
    I am sound personified.
    Exactly what a whisper would sound like,
    if it found out it was actually a scream.
    Imagine how big it would stand,
    if it knew it was a standing ovation,
    but then again,
    this is all just speculation.

I don't know where I come from.
    Let my bones tell it,
    I'm the daughter of rage.
    Some days I can catch myself right before the implosion,
    but every so often,
    my combustion is inevitable.
    I feel it run up and down my body,
    until it collides with the bend of my knee,
    or the crease of my elbow.
    But even when it ends,
    it never stops.

I don't know where I come from.
   Is this all of me?
   Is the weight of my wholeness on this frame,
   the entirety of me?
   Maybe one day I'll meet the version of me they keep waiting for.
   The one that lives up to expectations,
   and carries the world with no complaints.
   Instead, I'm constantly crushed under the weight of my own mind,
   but maybe, just maybe,
   I'll be able to put it down and let it live alone.

I don't know where I come from,
   and I probably never will.
   Maybe I'll tell my niece I came out the belly of a whale,
   or was the animal Noah forgot.
   Maybe I'll skip over the years where life felt worthless,
   and jump to my favorite love story.
   The one where I am lifted and loved back.
   Or maybe, just maybe,
   I'll spill the beans on me being as lost today as I was at 5 years old,
   so that she'll know she comes from a long line,
   of self-discovery.
   & she'll take pride in being lost,
   because we always find our way back home.

Backstroke

"I swam in the belly of a beast, and you could not tell me I wasn't in paradise. There's a reason the acid didn't burn me."

C/eserean

My mother swelled so bad in the hospital,
   she refused pictures.
   No desire to archive the moment.
   She felt pain,
   like she felt breathing.
   It was nothing new,
   but then again it was.

Her belly stretched her frame to a new form.
   Her nose reached from ear to ear.
   Calves like elephants,
   hands like mitts,
   she was preparing to catch me.
   Lap after lap she walked and half dragged us around that hospital.
   19 years my senior,
   she entered the world in that same place.
   Those same walls that held her first cry,
   would hold mine.
   Those walls would sing our first song together.

An hour before the sun would set,
   her screams were the horns that welcomed me.

There was no clear entryway,
I was born through a wound.
Snatched from in between her organs,
covered in blood and bodily fluids.
She couldn't even watch me come earthside,
and so would be the nature of our relationship.

We stand in a constant state of disconnect.
    19 years between person to person can feel like a valley,
    but between mother and daughter it is a blink.
    It is less than a blink, it is actually no collapse of time.
    You knew mother before you knew woman,
    & your exhaustion is valid,
    I just wish you had more strength to carry me.
    But, is that too much to ask after you carried me?

Mama do you know how many times you almost buried me?
    How many times our goodbyes were almost final?
    In your shadows I made fires but they never kept me warm.
    Had food that filled my belly but I was never full.
    Had 'I love you's leave tongues, enter ears, but never settle in me.
    'I love you' nauseated me to the point of shaking,
    but I still chased it wanting that feeling,
    because the nothing in its place nearly starved me.

I've known you as mother, caretaker, provider,
    but to know you as woman,
    is to know you separate from me.
    & with you being so far away already, that terrifies me.
    What were your dreams before me?
    What parts of you do you wish you could explore just as yourself?

What healing did you put on pause to assume a role?
What was killed in you to give me life?

The woman in me desires answers, but the daughter in me,
   yet, the little girl in me, enjoys the veil.
   She still remembers Mrs. Fields cookies on Saturdays.
   Matching outfits for 1-hour photos.
   Daydreams of growing up to be just like you,
   but this woman,
   mama this woman feels deeply what you didn't heal.
   She has flashbacks to tear-filled nights longing for you.
   Sitting across from you with a broken heart in her chest,
   and you never noticing.
   You watched my every move but never noticed me.

You don't see how hard I work,
   to dismantle the 'could have been's we hold.
   How I hold my breath and jump into murky waters daily,
   praying that I learn how to swim on my way down.
   Sometimes, I jump just to see if you will come after me.
   Mama I never saw the noose slipped around your neck,
   but I've seen you jump for me.
   My spirit threw tantrums yelling for you to see me.
   Me today.
   Me presently.
   Me as woman,
   but you are still just mama to me.
   I guess,
   I truly am my mother's daughter.

Quarter Breath

"I'm 25 still learning how to exhale. I pray to breathe evenly before I die. Some never do."

Miss. Luis Land

Ms. rickety bones.
   I hear you crack each morning,
   and break each night,
   but still you wake.
   Held together simply by faith,
   and on your worse day, duct tape.
   How you make your body move,
   when it's stiff to the point of pain?
   Where did you learn to suffer,
   and still progress?
   To shrink,
   but still be loud?
   To carry,
   but still be let down?
   I know so many women like you.
   I be women like you,
   but won't admit it.
   Supposedly I'm supposed to be a version built upon you.
   New and improved,
   the better.
   But I feel heavy just like you,
   with half the resilience.

BLACK GIRL FLESH

Truth is, I don't want to be resilient.
I want to exist without comparing scars.
Is my story less valid if it don't consist of war?
Can I only be satiated by tears?
Maybe, I'm not thirsty enough.
Maybe, I don't have enough disgust,
in the parts of me that be robust,
mainly my ego.
They still got closets from the 60's they wish to stuff me in.
Garments for mammy they want me to drown in.
They still, pushing the lie that I be less.
But I,
knowing more than most,
know,
humility was never a garment.
My skin was never a sin,
and my existence is revolutionary enough.

On a Sunday, or Monday

"Every time I take a step towards my own healing, my spirit breaks out into a praise dance."

Can't Ring Me Up

I got so many parts of me still hiding.
    Praying and hoping to never be discovered.
    Eating flesh to stay alive because my fruit trees are barren.
    Exploding with rage because I don't display my trauma no more.
    My body never knew normal,
    so this normal is bitter.
    Strange, unfamiliar, and terrifying,
    and is exactly why I love how deeply I feel.
    Emotions sprint out of my mouth every time it opens.
    I learned to train my words long ago.
    They begged me.
    They don't want to live in people who are temporary.
    They want us to preserve ourself.
    Only open up for self exploration.
    & I agree.
    I lent out parts of my self that I never got back,
    so now,
    this store is closed.

It's In You

"I'll never police who gets to be themselves. We all deserve the peace of being."

Textured Skin

I've had acne for as long as I've had skin to be judged. I've had deep craters you could swim in living on the borders of my laugh lines. Red blotches covered my cheeks for months on end. Had enough blackheads in the bridge of my nose to alarm white folks. My skin was a breeding ground for bacteria, which made my mind a playground for self-hate. Mirrors became my enemy. They always looked at me like they knew best. They judged me. Even when what they showed me felt as bad as it looked, something still told me there was more. Even with all the scars that ran down my face. The black circles that ran laps around my eyes. My uneven skin taunted me. It stared at me. Dared me to look at it and for years, I never did.

I was told I was beautiful but that word hung its self from the edge of my own lips. It never got far with me. They always lied to me. My emotions always jumped when anyone made mention of my skin. They didn't know what it was like to live with my face. To squeeze it, and pinch it. To burn it with intention hoping it would release. Begging it to be kind to me. Couldn't it see I was loving on it? All be it roughly, still love all the same. I scrubbed it meanly at times, but I still loved it all the same. I could've loved it so much more if it would just listen. If it stopped rebelling. If it would just stop looking like an unloved child, but it wouldn't. It demanded that I see it as it was.

It took years for me to look at it and say "I see you", but one day I finally did. I saw it trying. Fighting. Having moments of clarity, but still falling short. My skin was just the me I pretended not to see. It was a lot braver than me because it had no choice. Where could it go and not be seen? Be walked past and not be noticed? A Black face, with textured skin, has nowhere to hide. As soon as my eyes pop open in the morning, it is on display. I had to learn to live with skin that spoke for me. To be gentle with a face that was stubborn. I had to love what even I declared as unloveable. Isn't it ironic? That my greatest teacher of self-love would be blackheads and marks, red patches, and textured skin.

A Bag Full of Bricks

I found joy in a well-healed scar from my childhood. I remember the day I got it. I was in St. Luis playing games with little girls from the neighborhood my Grandmother grew up in. It was my turn to run, and I jumped off the bricks that lined the front yard, and landed on both hands and knees. I was a rough child, so I barely even noticed. I just got up and kept running till my Grandma saw me wild-haired, with blood running down my leg to my socks. She cared way more than I did, but I still stopped and let her clean me up. This was the theme of my childhood. Me running wild with no sense of direction. Bumping into things and never even stopping to acknowledge the pain. Eventually, someone would come and clean me up. I never even cared about the scars that were left behind, I just liked the feeling of being free.

Freedom comes at a price. Although some pay a monetary amount, many pay their weight in flesh or in silence. If you would have asked me as a teenager "Who bought your freedom?", I would've stared at you squarely and answered "Me". Wouldn't have thought about it twice. Nobody else was living that life and enduring that trauma, so yes, I bought my own freedom. More so, my right to be free. I would've said that with a straight face then. I can't help but laugh now. Little girl what did you know about sacrifice? Yes, you carried things that no girl your age should have, but at least at that time, it was just yourself you carried. You didn't know how light you were. You felt small but trust me, you were much bigger than what you thought because of the shoulders you stood on. I can't speak for Black women across the world, but I knew for me, I walked through life for a long time with an empty bag.

My mom began adding bricks to her bag in '75. She was also born in '75. Her mother came into the world with a bag full of bricks, just waiting for her to be strong enough to carry them. My father's mother had a bag with a few less bricks on the day she was born, but I'm sure it was still just as heavy. The weight these women carried bought my freedom. They bought it before My grandmothers even formed in my great grandmother's wombs. They paid for my freedom blindly, with no receipt, & no return policy. They just got what they got, and every day, I work to be worth it. There was a time I didn't realize or appreciate what these women paid for me, but now, with my own bag getting heavier and heavier each day, I thank God for the strength of their shoulders.

II

Blood

Stone Fruit

Apricot.
   Mango.
   Cherry.
   Nubs at the center.
   Ripe sweetness around them.
   Juices that escape the lips,
   & drip down the chin.

Pink.
   Red.
   Blush.
   Soft colors that scream femininity.
   Two-tone homes for admiring.
   Bold, yet subtle.
   Pungent, yet sweet.
   Pillar of life, yet addicting.
   How oxymoronic.

Smooth.
   Rough.
   Tender.
   As gentle as rose petals,

but handled like live grenades.
Stolen like petty candy,
but it is worth its weight in gold.

Clenched.
   Open.
   Valley.
   Running circles but staying still.
   A landing spot for the lost.
   Baptismal for the found.
   A new meaning for safe space,
   but a safe space it is not.

Hers.
   Theirs.
   Mine.
   A whole portal,
   but those who hold it called mere mortals.
   There be more than magic here.
   There be suppleness.
   Fruit that hang high,
   orifices that gape,
   mouths that water,
   but it won't be devoured.
   It is a protest.
   It will die defiant.
   You will never know its sweet relief.

Abyss

"The first time I felt love so deep I thought I would drown, I found it crawling in a Black woman, & I never crawled back out."

Luther Let Me Sang

If this world were mine
    I'd hide my mask.
    My need to be needed.
    My want to be wanted.
    See my hideout would be hiding out,
    and I could only present myself in plain sight.
    Finally, they could see me.
    I had to exhaust the exhaustion,
    that comes from always having to be "on".
    Lucky for us, in the privacy of our own homes,
    there is no need to perform.
    We're our whole selves and nothing else.
    Ain't enough brick to half step,
    see we stepping into a new space now.
    If this world were mine,
    I'd make it so that we'd never have to hide again.
    Make it so that we never have to worry about who was enemy or friend.
    Make it so that we actually lived in a country that we wouldn't mind,
    placing our hands over our hearts for.
    In real allegiance, in true alliance.
    All quilted together by defiance.
    If this world were mine,

LUTHER LET ME SANG

I'd make it so that everybody,
could get the food the body actually deserves.
Make it so that our home and our houses were one and the same.
Evictions, only to the spectators.
Land, back to the natives.
Money for all the creatives.
No more starving artist,
in this world I call my own.
See, I'd make it so that we'd no longer have to hide away in corners,
taking table scraps of whatever they want to give us.
No more need for us to constantly have mask,
even where we are "accepted",
or where we "should" feel comfortable.
Mask off.
24/7, 365,
if this world were mine.

Fairy Tales for Black Girls

"I pray for happy endings for all the Black women who never saw one. You deserve to be the first. You deserve partnerships that encompass your heart's desires if you want. Fulfillment within yourself, regardless. Your reality deserves to feel like a dream too."

Amerikkkan Pie

I guess I'll be yo picnic table.
  For yo apple pie,
    yo lemon cake & paper plates.
  A cooler for your cokes,
    and a dispenser for your pink lemonade.
  Oh, wait.
I guess it ain't as sweet when you got to ask for it.
You a sneaky pie type of guy.
Like yo slices with superiority and no space for no's.
You always need a little something sweet, don't you?
Oh, I ain't yo type.
You ain't know I was the fireworks on 4th of July?
The embers that light up the grill,
  or the bonfire.
I'm that fire that sits behind your pupils of the good ole days,
  but, I'm not the one getting hung up on words.
I bleed red, lack white, and I'm blue in the face from all the screaming.
Value my Black berry that's juicer than most,
  more than they know,
  & they got the nerve to think I'm the one walking around cloaked.
Like I'm scared of being the bad guy,
  but ain't I already?

Don't I take up real estate in your mind?
Must got a cute cottage, with a front-yard filled with sunflowers,
& you must hate sunflowers,
like you hate me.
Got a real pit in your stomach that I keep making deeper,
and deeper.
So deep you forgot what it means to be full.
I hope a slice of cake never satiates your sweet tooth again.
You only deserve spoonfuls of salt,
til yo tongue dries up & begs for water.
May you never, have your thirst quenched again.

The Collective

"The pain is collective, but so is the joy."

I Really Am Just Human

Is me as human not enough for you?
    Me standing simply in front of you don't excite you?
    You don't feel the privilege of seeing my humanity as you should.
    It's not a magic potion that flows through my veins,
    or leaks out of me every 28 days.
    In alignment with the moon,
    so I get the confusion,
    but it really is just blood.

Cycles of The Moon

"I bleed but don't die every month. Maybe I am that magic they speak of."

My Own Wonderland

I cut my own skin to bathe in the rivers of my blood.
   Hoping to finally be fully submerged within myself for once,
   instead of only feeling my skin through someone else's fingertips.
   I ran through my hair wildly.
   I felt and admired each coil,
   and got lost in the complexities of my own kinks,
   but still felt found and grounded.
   I swam in the brown of my iris',
   and stood starstruck of my own twinkle.
   I allowed myself to be the center of my own attention,
   instead of begging to be seen.
   I made hammocks of my ear lobes for me to lay on,
   to exhale in,
   and to, for once, hear myself first.
   I swallowed myself whole and slid down my insides,
   and was able to sunbathe in my own light.
   I didn't have to worry about outshining him.
   I placed two fingers in my sacred place,
   got on my knees and prayed to my own divinity.
   I thanked the God within me, for me,
   and my ability to see beauty in all the places I once tried to hide.
   I got to explore me as an ecosystem,

after spending a lifetime thinking I was just a pond.
Just a small collection of water,
in a world so much bigger than me,
but I am a world.
A world of my own,
and I love it here.

Cast a Spell When I Want To

"My magic can't be stripped. I simply choose when I allow you to claim it over me."

Gore, Wetness, & Weeping

I've spent most of my life happily standing in the background of others. Clapping for their wins, shedding tears at their love, and my spirit being fed in most parts. But, there were parts of me that longed to know a life without the overcast of everyone else's shadow. To be able to stand in the sun's light, and not through the filters of those who dared to feel it first. I always wanted to speak directly to the sun and let its warmth be the response. Fear placed me in a corner where the light couldn't reach me and I stayed there. Why? Who knows. Maybe it wasn't so bad to only feel the sun when it bounced off the skin of others. I was warm enough. Not too hot, or too cold, but then again, maybe I settled and became ok with not being able to choose. It could've been worse. I don't know that that worse is, but I'm told it could've been worse.

It was never about having my face be first or in front. I never cared about being "it", or the status quo. Honestly, I just wanted to possess the bravery to do both. To stand behind those I love and not feel less than, or, to stay in front of them without being perceived as better than. I wanted the duality to do both seamlessly. Everything inside me threw tantrums when I forced myself to sit in moments I should've stood, if for nothing else, myself. I was so worried about what people would think if I for once, just once, let myself be the center of my own attention. I was scared that the spotlight would shine light on me being far more broken than I thought. I thought it would be a magnifying glass to things I claimed were healed, and I was right.

The foreground has its perks, but it's not exempt from darkness. The difference is, the darkness seeps through cracks instead of appearing as a hole. When I looked at myself in a mirror after allowing myself into the foreground, even in just my own mind, I saw myself in a new light that was unforgiving. I saw cracks, dents, and holes that I never noticed before. I know some people become knowledgeable of their shortcomings, and choose to ignore them. Spending so much time in the shadows, it would have been easy for me, but I refused. I instead pried them open and made them bigger & deeper, deep enough for me to stand in. I can't tell you all that I found there, but know it was nothing I could ever forget. I spent time there. I learned why these pieces of me chose to be there. Some of them chose to come with me to this light-filled side, but some chose to stay there, and it was ok. I didn't need all of them to come with me. Honestly, it was probably better that they didn't. All parts of me don't need to be put on display for my whole self to be seen, and I can still present myself as complete. It didn't take much time or effort for me to reach a place where I could jump smoothly from light to dark, all it really took was the courage, which surprisingly I found, cared for, and nurtured in the shadows. Go figures.

With My Own Permission

"As a queer woman..." I said out loud for the first time for ears not just attached to my own head. I said it and paused internally for just a minute. It felt a lot lighter than I expected it to. I just knew if I let someone else hear it, I'd be gagged right then and there. Maybe they would throw a bag over my head and drag me to somewhere dark and leave me there until I took it back. And knowing me, there was a time I might've took it back. I had made leaps and bounds from that 16-year-old girl who tasted stone fruit for the first time. I had made love to and been loved by several women in those 10 years. I had acknowledged my sexuality, and even discussed it with people who I knew, just no one who ran in circles I frequented. I wasn't fearful of people finding out, but I always wanted the perfect time, and she was it.

I could not contain my smile at that moment. I laughed at myself for feeling so giddy, but she made me not embarrassed to have a child-like reaction. Plus, I could see her own smile deepening. Her shoulders released and we settled into the conversation, which unbeknownst to her, was unlocking another level of my self-discovery. For the first time, I was sitting as my whole self, all at once. It felt good and very right. For a while I associated this joy I felt with her being in my presence, and although she absolutely brought me joy, it was deeper than that. I had spent months prior to this moment rebuilding my sense of self I had let someone make me doubt. I spent a lot of time alone and asked myself questions. I still don't know why I thought my self-worth was safer in the hands of others. Why completeness frightened me. I asked myself a million questions, but came up with the same answer more often than not, "You are not yourself." It would repeat in my mind for hours at night. Kept me from sleeping. Made silence feel like punishment, so I made myself comfortable with noise.

When I first tried to interpret this message, I took it as literal. Was I just pretending to be this healing and whole person? Although I said I didn't want perfection, was it true? Was I, me, my being the lie? Those questions never stirred up answers within me. I still heard it every single day, "you are not yourself." I then just ran from it. Built a life where I was so damn busy I couldn't even find the time to think about it. Even flew 7,000 miles across the world to get away from it, only to still find it in my head. I climbed to the top of a mountain, real biblical like, and asked God what was I missing? What did I not see? Then, I finally heard it. "You are not yourself, but you can be." I was never missing anything. Wasn't incomplete. Didn't need validation from anyone outside of me. All I ever needed was to give myself permission, and with God in my ear that day, I finally did. I met her 1 week from that day. She was the first person I really had spoken to since then, and when I opened my mouth to speak to her, I spoke with new words, with my own permission.

III

Body

The Audacity of This...

I feel complete.
    Comfortable in my own skin.
    I wake up and speak life into me.
    The sun kisses parts of me most will never truly know exist.
    I save a me for myself that only comes out when I lure it with joy.

I am whole.
    They told me I shouldn't be.
    Black women barely free,
    & Black women like me ain't supposed to be next in line.
    Then here I come sauntering in,
    with all of me out,
    & they don't know what to do with me.

I am.
    The fullness of me from the plump of my toes,
    to the chunk around my knees.
    A fat Black woman with audacity.
    They always attempt to chop me down to size.
    They say I got too much of it,
    but I just come back time and time again,
    like the root I am.

You could never get rid of me.

Frame Me Free

"My body loves freedom more than my mind. Go figure."

Homebound

I spoke with God.
   They told me I have parts of me hidden so deeply,
   that I could never find them.
   They told me,
   although my heart swears solitude is the sweet relief I always wanted,
   I was doing a disservice to myself by hiding in plain sight.
   Where I was meant to go,
   I could not go alone.
   My fear was always other people.
   I never set out to break my own spirit,
   although I broke my own heart plenty of times.
   I was a martyr for love.
   I once thought it to be so literal,
   but it takes on many forms,
   & the one that lived in others,
   always seem to hurt the most.
   I was 23 before I realized that a body could be love.
   It was not limited to the heart.
   My grandmother didn't lie when she said,
   I should be loved from head to toe,
   but she left out the part where I should thank my body too.
   My feet carrying me after I forced them into cheap,

HOMEBOUND

too small shoes,
is love.
My knees holding strong as I praise the ancestors,
with a shake that emits from my core,
is love.
My elbows holding up my head,
and sacrificing their suppleness to support me,
is love.
The fact that my body continues to move through this world with me,
even when it's crucified at every turn,
proves that it is the deepest love I will ever know.
So no, I wanted no parts in it being a home for anyone else.
They don't love it like it loves me,
and it's obvious.
But God,
I think I get it now.
I thought you wanted me to plant seeds of myself in others,
& anxiously wait for what could grow there,
ignoring the piece of earth I am.
Homes,
can only be built on land that is cleared.
I was never really alone because I was by myself,
I was alone because I made space for lonely,
when home,
is what I've been for so many others,
but home,
I was never for myself,
but I could be.
What if I took my body everywhere I went?
What if, instead of me opening my front door for every knock,
I enjoyed the peace of being alone?

What if, home and body had the same address?
What if I never had to ask myself what if again?
For this body, I've been to war,
& with it, I will die,
and every day within it,
I live.

The Good Steward

"By being a steward to my purpose, I've cultivated the power to tell my own story."

Swallow Whole

I always been one to take on the world,
    swallow by swallow,
    instead of,
    bite by bite.
    I guess to me it's all one and the same.
    An ends to a means,
    but every time I'm still shocked when I begin to choke.

Infinite Me

"In the universe, I take up as much space as I need, & there are no complaints."

Veins Be a Wiretap

I wish I could walk outside without being in someone's captivity.
    Without spending my mornings prepping for the battle the day held.
    Every day seems to be an uphill battle.
    I want a day where I can get dressed and not think of what it all means.
    A simple dress and chunky earrings because they make me smile,
    and glasses for the sun and not to hide myself.

There is no outside that is safe for me.
    I work overtime just to make my inside a place where I can exhale.
    Countless times I've held my breath for whole days.
    For weeks at a time my chest knew no release.
    A misstep, or the right step, could send me to the land of no return,
    where I would be in plenty company of women who look just like me.

They wouldn't come find me.
    They never come find us.
    Guess we ain't worth the first or second look.
    We go missing, and they go silent.
    We die, and they go silent.
    We exist, and they go silent.

We deserve outcries that are heard.

The riots with allies on the frontlines,
and all the sacrifices,
but not if they are only cut from our skin.
We don't have enough bones for rattling,
or tongues for lashing.
Our existence should matter to you too.

Heavy isn't it?
   Now carry it for 80 years.
   Then add your mother's, and her mother's, and her mother's,
   until you have generations of weight on your back.
   I'm glad it feels heavy.
   It should be way lighter for us,
   or at least not break our backs,
   since unlike you,
   we never get to put it down.

Watch Me Riot

"My body is no place for a riot, but it will if it must."

My Body Bag

I haphazardly throw my body around.
   I disregard that it knows pain.
   I've seen it turn colors right before my eyes,
   but to bruise means to feel,
   and numbness is more friend than foe now.
   It has its own mannerisms.
   It knows when to clench.
   How to contort itself into something a little less scary.
   Less intimidating,
   more female,
   less woman,
   barely human.
   The only sign of life it is allowed is bated breath,
   as it anxiously awaits its inevitable swallowing whole.

My body knows how to be "good".
   It bites inner cheeks when tongue begs to defend it,
   because it knows,
   meekness gives better odds for survival,
   but even silence can't save it.
   It is seen as a threat.
   People hear it screeching at all hours of the night,

but my ears must have fallen deaf to it.
As I sleep,
it must grow 30 inches and crawl through sewers,
linger just a little too long in doorways.
It is a menace to society.

My body is not allowed to be soft in any context.
    Its exterior and interior are demanded to be rough.
    To be fixed with sharp edges.
    To gape instead of exhale.
    Through wounds is the only way it is permitted to be open.
    Through tears is the only way it can release.
    Pain is the only emotion it can exude on the regular,
    that no one stands in protest of.

My body is seen as excessive.
    As though it bore a shape before this one.
    Like it broke a mold that it didn't know it was supposed to fit in.
    With infinite space, it still somehow is too much.
    Bursting at the seams every chance it gets,
    because it knows,
    boxes are too close to coffins,
    and conforming is death of the spirit,
    but as long as it resists,
    It.
    Is.
    Not.
    Dead.
    Yet.

#FreeMyWords

"With two hands wrapped around my neck, I still speak as I please. My words can not be caged."

Dancing With Two Fat Feet

To love my fat body is to love its obesity. Its stretched skin and cellulite. To love it as grand, even when it's made to feel small. I have learned to love it even when it is gawked at in disgust. I have to. It begs me to, and though I once responded to it with starvation, I now respond to it with nurturing and care. I know that it is stronger because of it by the way it opens up now. My mind and it speak only with tones of love. Neither one attacks the other for folding into its self, or for wanting to be heard and seen. They know how tight and crippling shrinking feels, and demand to be expansive.

I know there are many negative connotations with fat. By those who were never, and those who are always. It is the heaviest 3 letter word I know, right next to die and cut. It is seen as obscene and mean, but it is only a word to me. A descriptor of my physical. A word that no longer hurts me. I am fat. I am fat and Black. I am fat, Black, and a woman. I am expected to hate all parts of this description. I'm supposed to run away from it until I lose the weight I'm crucified for, but I don't. In fact, I love it with even more intention because of how hated it is.

I grab my love handles and dance with them. I smile till my double chin is prominent. I laugh until my belly jiggles. Where others see dips in skin and hanging fat from arms, I see a constant reminder that I am soft and pliable. I can always be transformed and molded into a better version of myself. There are people who think loving a fat body is being complacent. As though it is inherently wrong to love what we are in spite of. I'll love this body as it is fat. If it becomes thin, I will love this body as it is thin. If it becomes sick and frail, I will love this body as sick and frail. There is no form of it that is more or less deserving of my love. My body is more than the weight it carries. It as a spirit with a heart too, that is focused on loving every inch of it, and celebrating everyday it gets up to fight again.

Mental Gymnastics

I have days that I'm not ok. Where I'd rather do anything under the sun than to be present with myself. I've had more days trying to figure out what was wrong with me, than days of me feeling I was fine. To feel comfortable is a rarity for me, but it still happens more now than ever. Growing up I thought I was just moody. All throughout my teenage years I had a bad attitude and felt like angry was just my personality. Disappointments were my normal and even with low expectations, my needs just weren't met. I barely remember High School because I spent most of it in my own head. Always worrying about the optics of myself. Was I too much? Too little? Do I appear as to expansive? Or microscopic? I spent so many hours wondering what people thought of me that I never took the time to develop an opinion of myself.

For a while, I thought everyone hated themselves. I thought everyone spent nights convincing themselves that nobody cared about them or wanted them around. Weren't we all convinced that we didn't matter? In High School, maybe, at 25, no. Although it was not just me, it shouldn't have been anyone. I didn't realize the dips and dives my mental health took as a teenager, until I was an adult who willingly went to therapy. Therapy with another Black woman cracked my world wide open. It exposed the false normalcies I adapted to. The gymnastics my mind did to explain away my logic. I didn't realize I spent my life in a mental prison that I didn't want to be paroled from. I made comfort out of cement floors and family of guards that depended on my captivity. So much so, that even the mention of freedom terrified me. I was a real-life Biscuit at the gun line. Death felt less scary than me actually being myself. Those days spent in the swamps of my mind were rough, but they were the catalyst to me building out a life where freedom felt free.

Being myself has been my life's work. It takes an incredible amount of patience, understanding, and gentleness that was not innate in me. I came from an incomplete childhood at best, where I spent more time alone than anything. I developed a comfort with my physical self, but my mental took advantage. It didn't give me the space within it I needed to become a well-rounded person. Sometimes I think there are no well-rounded people, just people who avoid the dark corners of themselves, but I still strive to be as round as possible. Right now, I can bend at times. Sometimes I can even contort myself into a U shape, but it's always forced and temporary. I'm still working on having a life that moves seamlessly in a circular motion, but I still congratulate myself for trying. For acknowledging how up and down my life has been, but not forcing steadiness on the seesaw. For letting it be up and down without reverting back to a version of me that enjoyed it. I don't know if I'll get to that ideal place I now have trained my mind to envision, but at the very least, I'm dedicated to doing the work. For that, and all the moments I felt stretched thin, that I now see as growth, I am proud. Proud that I sifted through pounds and pounds of self-doubt, and found the courage to tackle my own mind.

IV

Heart

Love, of Course

I've known a world without it.
   It felt like a never-ending winter.
   Never thought I'd see the leaves change color again,
   let alone, the flowers bloom.
   Had a hard time envisioning the sun,
   wanting to caress my face like it once did.
   My perception was warped into believing,
   I enjoyed the icy solitude,
   even when my body found itself rebelling,
   from the lack of intimacy.

I once felt a love where love was absent.
   In its place was guilt dressed up just like it.
   Telling me the things it once did.
   The sweet nothings lost their sweetness.
   They became like vapor around me,
   and my muscle memory tricked me into believing I was satisfied.
   But the hollowness of the words,
   echoed within me.
   I can still feel them hitting against my rib cage,
   and creating a vibration,
   I swore I could hear.

Silence is too heavy a weight for me to bear.
   To be soothed and caressed by lies, I'd rather be.
   Does that make me the masochist to your narcissist?
   I yearn for your gratification even at the hands of my own undoing.
   You need for me to see you as needed,
   without being able to depend on you.
   We both somehow thrive on my own pain,
   but only one of us is deserving to,
   and I can't decide which one of us it is.

I once knew a world without you.
   The ground was shaky,
   and threatened to cave under me with every step,
   but it felt more whole than you.
   Even at the parts it disconnected at,
   I still knew I could place my full weight downward with each step.
   I don't know that to be true with you.
   I see an abyss in your eyes,
   but still feel your hands,
   and don't know which one is lying to me.

There's a home after you.
   I see it clear as day when I allow my eyes to close.
   I taste it,
   I feel it,
   tangibly within my arms reach.
   My fingertips beg to hold on to something worth holding for once.
   To hold something that will hold me back,
   but not in the ways you do.
   My senses come alive at the thought of being out of your grasp.

LOVE, OF COURSE

No longer hungrily waiting for you to amuse them.
I know I can't hold you and all of this at once.
Something must fall,
and It can't be me this time.

Shrunken

"I am no longer shrinking myself to stand behind men that I am better than."

Music Holds Memories

Melodic words with snaps and base transport me.
    Take me to a place with people who I've yet to mourn.
    Knowing they still draw breath,
    makes it that much harder.
    No one teaches you to grieve those who are gone,
    but won't leave your spirit.
    Who are a phone call away,
    but will never give you the answers.
    Severed from us,
    without closure.
    How has it come to a point where you,
    hold space in my heart,
    but we can't hold a conversation?
    Memories of you hit me like dreams of my grandmother.
    They're the only way we speak now.
    Lyrics were always our scripts for times we couldn't perform,
    now they are our relics.
    I hear them and think of what used to be.
    Do you know how many songs I've laid to rest,
    because I couldn't handle the memories they hold?
    How cemented my body feels,
    when I cave and place them on indefinite repeat.

because hearing them is the only way I let myself acknowledge,
there was once an us, in love.
Those words feel so foreign now,
but I still know exactly what they mean.
You were the first portal I explored that wasn't my own.
My first home away from home,
& somehow, through it all,
I'm still a home for you.
Am I, still a home for you?
Today I feel like a graveyard with holes dug,
but only warm bodies present.
Flowers that are still blooming,
with no desire to wilt or be dried.
Cold slabs of marble,
with no years of death marked.
I guess my heart won't let me grieve,
what it feels hasn't died yet.

& Again

"The most high has handcrafted a multitude of loves for me, & if this one doesn't work, I will love and be loved again, and again, until it feels right."

House of Worship

Fat Black bodies be temples too.
   Just as they are,
   you can clap for them.
   You can even admire them without that twinge of guilt,
   or embarrassment someone told you you should have.
   Why?
   Because fat Black bodies only deserve acknowledgment,
   when it is married with ridicule.
   That's what someone told you,
   & you believed them.
   You regurgitate someone else's words,
   like they don't still leave a sour taste in your mouth.
   Like you won't be convicted for them,
   like you have committed no crime at all.

Love on fat Black bodies boldly,
   loudly,
   and in public.
   Love on them fiercely,
   and steadily,
   even when eyes that don't belong to you,
   cause that bubbling in your belly that makes you want to retreat.

HOUSE OF WORSHIP

Love them still.
Treat them like art,
to be preserved,
and when tarnished,
restored,
but love them first,
like the humans they are.

Sweet, Sweet Love

"I've never known sweetness like this, and I may never again. I'm glad this is enough."

Out of My Element

I am missing the calmness.
   The storm.
   The beach,
   and the hurricane.
   Never knew what I'd get with you,
   but it always brought us closer together.

We could sit in silence.
   In darkness.
   Lay in the sun,
   or cuddle up in the cold.
   The elements meant nothing.
   We created our own turns with the wind and landed where we landed.

I wish it was as simple as grass.
   As daisies in a field.
   The only water they see is morning dew,
   that kisses them coldly,
   after a greeting from the sun.
   I wish we could stand in open air,
   and feel steadiness once again.

It Is My Pleasure

"None of my pleasure is guilty, nor is pleasure debatable to me. My pleasure is a priority."

Diving In It

I jumped in a pool when I was six,
   unable to swim and scared to relax,
   I nearly drowned,
   & had to be saved.
   I coughed up water filled with chlorine for hours.
   but the next day,
   I jumped in again.

I dived into her pool when I was 25,
   able to swim and at peace like I've never felt before.
   I floated in her still and calm.
   I had never swam in waters this deep,
   but still at her surface I floated,
   still, and calm.
   Yet I still nearly drowned,
   & had to save myself.
   My body felt weak for days.
   but then a week later,
   I jumped in again.

Rejoice

"If I do not rejoice in the small victories of this world, life will swallow me whole."

My Own Magic

"I don't want to be magical," I said with a heart full of low expectations and still heavy disappointments. I was on the ropes again. Lost yet another fight with myself for lying like I always do when faced with my own power. I played with it. Twiddled it between my fingers, stared at it in them, wondering if it was real. Some days I felt it shoot right up from the earth into my feet. I could feel it travel through my body, settling right in my chest. Right in the space I kept my spirit in. It would jump for joy every time I used my tongue in its favor. It stays because I've mastered the art of saying spells poetically, and honor it every time I speak.

People treat you differently when they know you are special. They may not know exactly what it is, but they feel it. They feel a tingle when they hug you. A flooding of warmth when their hands connect with yours. They look into your eyes and their shoulders relax almost instantly. Your voice is soothing to them, and it feels good for the most part. It makes you feel wanted, needed, like you could make a difference with just your presence. It's what we all dream of, until it's not. Until those hugs began to feel like strangulation, and those hands hold on a little too tight. You'll look into their eyes and you won't find that comfort they found in yours. They'll be laced with good intentions, but they also don't mind walking away with a piece of you, and it wouldn't be so bad if it was only one person, but it never is.

People see power and assume strength. They don't always coincide with one another. Strength is built up over time. You get knocked down often enough from the shakiness of your knees, so you build them up by running. But power is innate, regardless if the body it lives in harnesses it or not. It still exist and people who lack it desperately seek it. Most of them don't realize that power, or magic, doesn't stop humans from being human. We still have pain we don't know what to do with. Still run into people who disregard us. Our minds and our bodies don't always benefit from our magic. They still break down. They still hurt. We are still just navigating through life as a human. As person. I'm just a woman too. Don't use my magic as an excuse to treat me as anything less than that. I will bleed like you. If I stop breathing, I will die like you. And if my body is forced to endure pain repeatedly, without time to rebuild its strength, it will break, just like you.

When Flowers Die

I like to let my roses die. I never think to put them in vases to prolong their life. I'd rather watch them wither away. Watch reds turn to pinks, then pinks turn to brown, until I finally choose to part ways with them. Living things bring me joy. They excite me in ways that my own existence could never, but there is something about watching a full cycle of life come to an end, without violence or struggle. This process has healed me in a way I didn't know was possible. I went a whole lifetime without seeing how death can breathe life into people. Where I come from and where I've been, life and death don't live as harmoniously.

When my flowers die, there is no sadness. There is no swelling in my chest or eyes that feel like they might burst any minute. I don't feel stuck, or feel that blanket of despair that I often feel when I watch life leave bodies. Instead, I thank them for the gift they were to me, and let them decompose. I think the difference is that a plucked rose knows it is on borrowed time. Black people know the same to be true, but we still plant faith in humanity that always lets us down. I've never known a Black life that had a full cycle of being planted, nurtured, blooming, and dying peacefully. Although, I can't think of a people who deserve it more.

I fantasize about a time where plucked black life is treated like and give as a gift. Where they can be placed in water, replanted, or able to have every petal fall when it is ready. When they arrive on doorsteps or in the hands of lovers, smiles would spread across faces, and the hands that receive them wouldn't think of them as heavy. They would sit in a window sill, on a dining room table, or atop a chest of drawers, living out their final moments being admired and adored. They'd be allowed to wilt in peace. No one would bother them for existing, and soon, for not existing. When their petals began to fall on the table or the floor, they would be allowed to, peacefully. Then, once they could no longer hold up their blooms, and their water went cloudy, they'd be removed from their vase. Most of them discarded, but not violently. Some parts of them turned into mulch to help other flowers bloom. Then some would be tucked away into heavy books to be keepsakes, and reminders of the gift they were.

V

Spirit

Last Respects

They may bring flowers.
    May come with fascinators fixed to freshly pressed hair.
    In black dresses with creases down the front,
    or maybe with large leather belts around the waist,
    and a brooch pinned to their chest.
    They may come with sweet words written in weathered notebooks,
    or their favorite memory jotted down on a napkin.
    But honestly, they may come with nothing to say at all.
    They may come to kiss both cheeks of your mother.
    To hold your father a way only men who knew him his whole life could.
    Might kiss the hand of your grandmother,
    or to see that your sister is still on her two feet.
    Some may come to hold your hand one last time.
    To **see** your physical one **last time**.
    To say goodbye,
    or to say I love you.
    They may come,
    and display a love you always wanted from them,
    but then again, they may not come at all.
    Love yourself regardless.

Lay a Rose

"And when I die, lay your words with your roses, so everyone can see what our love looked like."

A Couple Bodies

I've watched things turn sour far before their expiration date.
  Like milk.
  Like bodies.
  I know exactly what it looks like to see a body with no soul,
  both dead and alive.
  Bodies are vessels that carry spirits from one life to the next,
  but there is still something so spiritual about blood spilled.
  Something so sinister about watching a God body,
  be reduced to past tense.
  Their existence is just a blimp in our memories,
  but that pungent smell sticks with you forever.
  They are a reminder that bodies do more than hold.
  They are holy.

Lost Connection

"Never thought I'd miss a spirit's body this bad. The physical is out of touch"

I Could've Been Ugly

I could've been ugly.
   I could've listened to what they said beauty was.
   Unwound my self-worth and put it in a box.
   Packed away what made me, me.
   Hid behind nonexistent waist line,
   praying to fit a mold.
   But Instead,
   I yelled at God.

I remember,
   when I prayed to be ugly.
   When I wished my body would disappear,
   although I was uncertain it existed.
   Wished that the lust in their eyes,
   was replaced by the disgust in their words,
   & I could breathe again.
   I found myself folding into the rolls of me,
   folding into the roles of she,
   but I yelled at God.
   Cause even with doubt,
   I knew my life was more than what my body could endure.

BLACK GIRL FLESH

I begged for ugly,
   like I begged for no,
   like I begged for mercy,
   like I begged, & got nothing.
   I had to make a home out of emptiness.
   I had to love a body I tried to kill.
   I had to love a body that bruised like peaches,
   tore like paper,
   that never new the purity of white.
   It always knew black,
   as pain,
   as despair,
   as the never-ending story of begging for no.

I remember embracing ugly.
   Touch of bald head,
   & clothes that hid nothing.
   Obtuse and obese they were forced to see me.
   I swallowed their pride and mine,
   and chose the revolutionary position of whole.
   Beautiful still has trouble rolling off my lips.
   It gets stuck somewhere between,
   of course and as if,
   but my lack of acknowledgment,
   don't make it cease to exist.

I should've been ugly.
   How much easier it would have been,
   to hide in those moments sunlight felt like death.
   Would have saved someone much time on my eulogy.
   Way less titles and hats to mention,

I COULD'VE BEEN UGLY

because way less nerve would've meant way less me.
Could've saved myself the pain of un-contorting my perception of self.
It would have been easy.
Oh how easy fat Black girls seem to disappear,
but instead,
I talked to God,
and they talked back,
& said;
"You are not shadow,
You are.
You are.
You are."

10 Toes Down

"The wiggling of my toes is all the confirmation I need to know I am love."

[Redacted] Black Woman

I screamed until words no longer had form.
    They fumbled out my mouth like the first steps of a newborn giraffe.
    Rushed out of my spirit like the levees breaking.
    Flooded everything around me yet I remained dry.
    I became island.
    I became fort,
    & words became moat.
    I was numb.
    I screamed until my limbs grew weak.
    Until my knees lost strength.
    Until my belly muscles grew tired.
    The veins in my neck bulged and reddened.
    I was angry,
    & it felt good.
    Now I see why they shame us for it.

Sacrifice

"Black girls learn to sacrifice before they even know what it means."

Joyful, Joyful

This one sparks joy.
   In herself.
   In others.
   On her best day, tenfold.
   On her worst, enough.
   She feels like Jesus.
   Some days Peter.
   Some days Mary.
   Every day, holy.
   It is a sermon every time she speaks.
   She is the personification of a prayer.
   Say amen when you see her.
   God blessed her.

Gut Full of Happiness

"I have joy in the pit of my stomach, & I pray it lives in there forever."

The Void of Loss

And just like that, the tears fall. Without warning, they begin to flood my eyes, and form streams running down my face. I grab a tissue and pat my now red cheeks dry, but they still continue to fall. Today is just one of those days. I was moving through life like I always do, progressing, dare I say even thriving, then all of a sudden a wave of sadness came over me. I could feel myself folding inward, and at first, I attempted to push through. Thought keeping myself busy would make it pass quicker, but I didn't have the strength to keep that up for long. I eventually just sat with it and held myself as I experienced all the emotions. This has been life for me lately. I've had some of my highest highs, but reality always seems to come and crush my spirits, and the reality is that you're not here anymore.

Grief is one of those things you wish someone told you about. They mention it ever so cavalier when a loved one passes, but they never really tell you how it feels, how it grows, how it can plain eat away at you. We take a few days off work and are sent flowers with notes telling us not to hesitate to reach out if we need anything. For the most part they mean it, at least for the first few days or weeks. Eventually the world forgets you're in pain, but you don't, and you never will. 6 months later you might wake up feeling just like that first day. Every time the phone rings, you'll think its that phone call all over again. An unanswered text might just send panic through your body. It'll take a while for you to be able to exhale, but honestly, you may never again. The hardest part is making peace with that.

Loss is the heaviest thing I've ever had to carry. This bag has made permanent grooves in my shoulders. My spine now has a curve to it and I can't even walk straight no more. Even on days I feel good I can't ignore my lopsided steps. Loss has carved deep voids within me that wrap around. Some of them are so deep I swear I can hear the whistling of the wind within me. I think my loved ones who have transitioned sometimes make music with the echoes. A reminder that though they are gone from this realm, they are still with me. In a way, even closer than before, because we have a thread that is both internal and eternal. Hugs may be different, and for a while conversations may feel one-sided, but they are there. Not physically, and maybe to no one else, but they are where ever you are. We make space in this world for them by holding and honor ourselves. They make space for us in spirit by carrying the love we have for them. We create bonds that can never be severed. One of the few things that brings peace to my longing after loss.

Hair Heavy

I woke up and stared deeply into the mirror. I had a face full of stress acne, a tattered dress that I pulled out of the dirty clothes, and a head full of unwashed and uncombed hair. It was very easy for me to see the mess I had made of myself physically, but this stare down in the mirror wasn't about that. I looked past all of that and reached into my spirit. I had to talk to her. Things had been rough for a few weeks, and I couldn't stand it anymore. I asked her "Why we so heavy?" Then we sat. We sat so long our legs fell asleep, so then we stood. Stood so long our back began to hurt, so then we laid, & as we laid, our hair fell into our face, and she finally replied, "That's why."

I hopped up and headed to my bathroom. The mirror in there wanted to stare me down too, but I had found what I was looking for. I ran my fingers through my tightly coiled hair. I then separated it into four sections. I placed a clip into each one then exhaled. I grabbed a pair of scissors and began to cut. I promise you with each snip my spirit dropped ten pounds. I cut, and cut, and cut until I had a small fro I hadn't seen on myself in years. It was cute, but it wasn't enough. I still was carrying some weight that wasn't mine. I rushed out to my local drugstore and bought the best clippers they had to offer. I walked back into my bathroom and plugged them in. I took a deep breath and let the buzz of the clippers drown out my fear. Once I began shaving my head my spirit flew. I shaved, and I smiled, and I cried, and I smiled bigger. This was it. This was the weight I was carrying that made my feet feel like cement boots. My whole life I had hair people fawned over. They called it 'thick and pretty' but few knew how hair could weigh you down. Change how you're perceived, and how you perceive yourself, regardless of what it looks like. I felt a lightness I hadn't known in years.

Black women's hair is heavy. It's political. It's biblical. It's spiritual. It holds on to everything we swear we're letting go of. It has memories we've forgotten. It knows us better than most. It is crown, but sometimes that crown is made of thorns. Sometimes it hurts. It's easily ripped away from us. It feels our wrath often. I can't think of how many times I wanted it to be what it was not, and hated it when it rebelled. I hated how free it demanded to be, in fact I was jealous. How could an extension of me be free, when it was the boot on my neck keeping me chained to what they thought? Out of anger, I cut it before, and as processed hair hit the floor I felt the same. Still had shoulders to my ears, and eyes red from crying, nothing changed. But this time, oh this time, it fell and that pit in my stomach closed up. It fell and my neck wasn't so stiff anymore. It fell, and a level of discomfort within myself fell with it. It's as if God was my barber, and with each section cut, they anointed me. I looked back in that mirror, and my spirit laughed at me. "How do you feel?" she asked, and with one of those 32 teeth smiles I replied, "Light as a feather."

VI

The End

A Completed Cycle

& that's it.
  A body of work written by me.
  As real as any moment.
  As deep as I could go.
  As raw as all the cuts in this here flesh.
  I gave it all I had and then some,
  and I'm still smiling afterward.
  Probably because I wrote this simply for me,
  and not to chase the ever elusive perfection,
  so charge all mistakes to my head, and not my heart.
  To think I asked myself was it worth it at one point.
  Were these words important enough for immortality?
  Could I stretch myself wide enough for this,
  and still be able to snap back to me?
  The answer is, and always has been, yes.
  I'm just happy I let myself say it.

Give Thanks

"I will never denounce my magic, but I'm thankful for the space to be human, and the courage to finally be both."

About the Author

Malaysia 'Maud' Alcorn is a spoken word artist, writer, & event curator that hails from Oakland, California. Her work revolves around her experience as a Black woman moving, growing, and healing in spite of a society that tells her to do the opposite. She believes in radical authenticity and uses it as a way to connect herself with people around the world. Wether it is through her spoken word, writing workshops she host, or through the events she curates via her organization 'Gold Beams', Maud is constantly working to use her talents to be an asset to her community. Her work is, and will always be, a love letter to herself and the Black women that surround her. With her writing, she hopes to continue to bridge, build, and be community.

Follow her on instagram @Maud.Alcorn

To learn more about her writing, find out about upcoming performances, and all other information, check out her website MaudAlcorn.com

To learn more about the community work she is involved in, upcoming events she will be curating, and more info about her organization, check out GoldBeams.org

www.ingramcontent.com/pod-product-compliance
Lightning Source LLC
Chambersburg PA
CBHW021115080526
44587CB00010B/524